D1464471

Be Kind

First published in 2021 by Sparrowlegs
Text © Anupa Roper 2021
Illustrations © Beckie Clarke 2021

ISBN: 978-1-5272-8411-1

Follow the Sparrowlegs journey: www.instagram.com/miss_sparrowlegs
Sorryforbeingawkward illustrations: www.sorryforbeingawkward.co.uk

A catalogue for this book is available from the British Library.

sparrowlegs

Written by
Anupa Roper

Illustrated by
Beckie Clarke

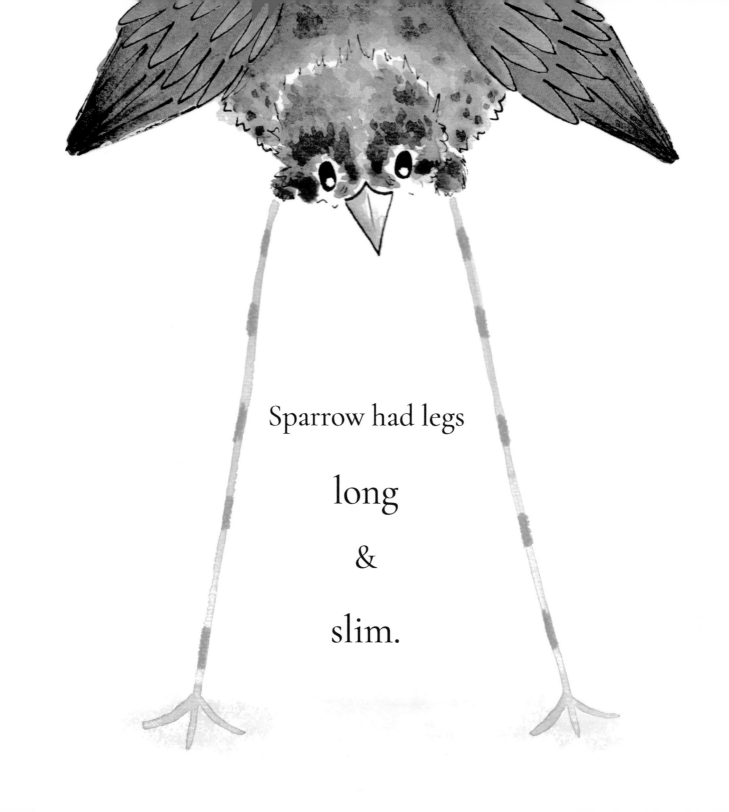

Sparrow had legs

long

&

slim.

Everyone called her skinny and thin.

This made her feel
so terribly sad.

Made her think that
her body was bad.

She sat for a while
and pondered...

"Why couldn't they see?"
she wondered.

That if they looked beyond her legs, they would find...

She was funny, she was kind.

Sparrow sat and thought one day.
She realised there must be another way.
So, up there in her favourite tree,
she thought of a new way to be.

Perhaps if she loved her body,
and all that it could do,
the others would see that,
and love her body too.

She embraced her amazing body.

Look what it could do!

She could fly up high on her wings,

use her voice to help her sing.

Her body is amazing.

Your body is amazing!

Every body is amazing!

You should love yours too.

Now Sparrow

has a

smile

on

her face.

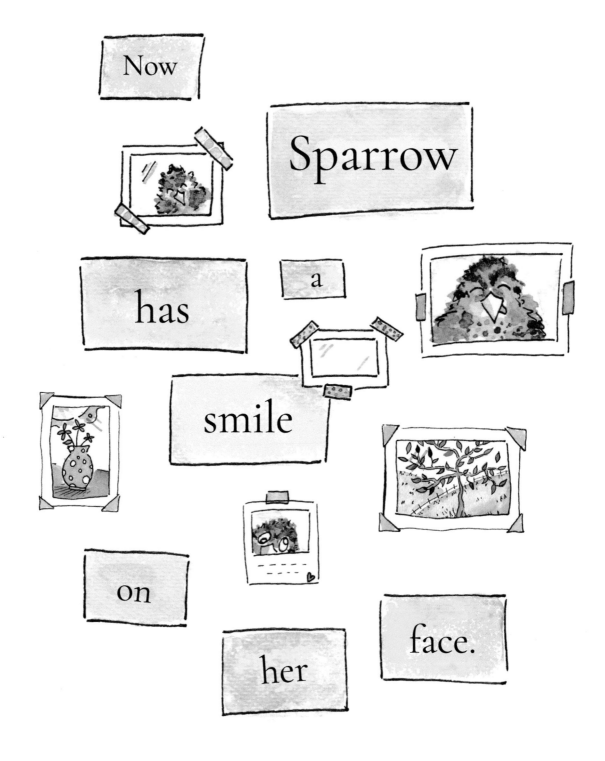

Her body is her home.

The perfect place.

At last,

Sparrow feels happy in her feathers.

Sparrow realised all that her body could do,
lots of things, not just a few!
She knew it was also time to begin,
appreciating her beauty within.

Printed in Great Britain
by Amazon